# THE VERDICT

## The Great Exchange That Closed the Case

LADELL WILSON

**The Verdict**
The Great Exchange That Closed the Case



All emphasis within Scripture quotations is added by the author unless otherwise indicated.

This book is intended for educational and spiritual growth purposes. It is not intended as legal advice, psychological counseling, or professional theological consultation. Readers are encouraged to seek appropriate counsel for specific personal needs.

First Edition
Printed in the United States of America

ISBN (Paperback): 979-8-9948705-2-5
ISBN (eBook): 979-8-9948705-3-2

## TABLE OF CONTENTS

*Having canceled the record of debt that stood against us with its legal demands, He set it aside, nailing it to the cross.*
*He disarmed the rulers and authorities and made a public spectacle of them, triumphing over them in it.*

Colossians 2:14–15

# INTRODUCTION

For generations, believers have lived as though the case were still open.

We have confessed, repented, fasted, pleaded, and rehearsed our failures as if Heaven were still deliberating. We have believed in forgiveness, yet operated as defendants. We have trusted in grace, yet lived as though we were still awaiting judgment.

But what if the hesitation is not in Heaven?

What if the ruling has already been rendered?

The cross of Jesus Christ was not a sentimental moment in history. It was not symbolic suffering meant merely to inspire devotion. It was a decisive and final legal event. Something happened there that did more than offer mercy. A verdict was issued.

From the beginning, Scripture reveals a courtroom narrative. There was delegated authority, covenant breach, lawful accusation, temporary covering, and a system that restrained judgment but never fully resolved the case. Humanity did not simply stumble morally. It entered legal exposure. Guilt created standing. Accusation found voice. Covering provided mercy, but the file remained open.

Until Christ.

Jesus did not come to negotiate terms.
He did not come to reduce a sentence.
He did not come to make forgiveness possible.

He came to close the case.

The blood of Christ did not merely cover sin as sacrifices once did. It canceled the record of debt. It removed the legal footing of the accuser. It satisfied justice without compromising mercy. When Jesus declared, "It is finished," He was not expressing exhaustion. He was announcing completion.

The verdict was in.

Yet many believers continue to live as though the proceedings are ongoing. Accusation still echoes. Shame still persuades. Striving still feels necessary. Not because the case remains open, but because the verdict has not been fully understood.

This book approaches the cross through a legal lens. It will walk carefully through Scripture to show how authority was granted, how breach occurred, how standing shifted, and how the cross resolved what covering could not. The language may feel structured, even deliberate, because the subject demands precision.

The cross did not begin a process.
It concluded one.

The question this book explores is not whether salvation is available. It is whether the ruling has been received. Not whether forgiveness is possible, but whether the case has truly been closed in our understanding.

Because if the verdict has been rendered, then there is no more trial.

And if there is no more trial, then we must learn to live as those who have already been acquitted.

## Chapter 1
# Jurisdiction

### What God Lawfully Granted to Man

Before we talk about what was lost, stolen, or recovered, we must establish the original jurisdiction. Who had legal authority on earth? By what right? Under what terms?

If the case is to be understood, we must begin where authority began.

### 1. Heaven's Government Model: Delegation, Not Occupation

God is Creator and King over all things. Yet in Genesis, He establishes a governing pattern rooted in delegation. The earth was not designed to be managed by angels, nor directly occupied by God in the same manner as heaven. God intended the earth to function under human stewardship. This was not symbolic language. It was a real grant of authority.

Genesis 1:26 contains legal language:

- "Let them have dominion..."
- "Over the earth..."
- "Over every living thing."

This was not permission to exist. It was jurisdictional assignment.

Dominion means:

- The lawful right to govern within assigned territory
- Authority to make decisions and enforce order

- Responsibility to cultivate and protect

In simple terms, God gave humanity real authority to steward the earth under His rule.

Human authority was not merely internal or moral. It was governmental. Humanity was created to represent heaven's rule within earth's boundaries.

### 2. Image and Likeness: The Credential of Authority

God did not give dominion to an anonymous creature. He gave dominion to an image bearer. Image and likeness function as a legal credential. In ancient cultures, when a king placed his image in a territory, it signaled ownership and authority.

When God created man in His image, He established:

- Representation
- Legitimacy
- Alignment to His rule

Man did not become God.
Man represented God within a defined jurisdiction.

Authority was not self-generated. It was delegated and relational.

### 3. The Garden Was a Legal Estate With Terms

Eden was not merely scenery. It was a domain of peace with structure and stipulation. God granted freedom, then established a boundary. Not because God is controlling, but because authority always functions under order.

Order does not reduce authority. Order protects it.

The command concerning the tree was not arbitrary. It served as:

- a covenant marker (will you trust My word?)
- a jurisdictional boundary (you are steward, not owner)
- a loyalty line (authority requires alignment)

The boundary did not reduce freedom. It defined rightful operation.

Authority without boundary becomes autonomy. Authority within boundary remains aligned.

**4. Adam as Federal Head: One Man Representing Many**

This is where the legal side gets heavy, but it is necessary.

Adam wasn't just "a guy." Adam functioned as a federal head. A representative whose actions could affect those under him. Scripture treats Adam as the head of humanity's earthly administration.

That's why later Scripture can say:

- "Through one man sin entered…" (Romans 5:12)
- "In Adam all die…" (1 Corinthians 15:22)

That's legal representation language: one authorized man, acting within a granted jurisdiction, affecting the estate.

**5. What God Gave Man (Legally)**

So, the original grant included:

- dominion (authority to steward the earth)
- access (fellowship with God without shame)
- identity (sonship/image-bearing legitimacy)
- inheritance (a world to cultivate)

- standing (no guilt, therefore no accusation)

And here's the key:
As long as man remained aligned, Satan had no legal claim in that jurisdiction. Meaning, the enemy had no rightful authority to interfere.

That's why the first battlefield wasn't physical. It was legal: word vs word, allegiance vs deception, covenant faithfulness vs breach.

Because if Satan could not take authority by force, he could only gain access by inducing a violation.

---

**What this chapter established (the legal thesis)**

1. God gave mankind lawful authority in the earth realm.
2. That authority was real jurisdiction, not symbolism.
3. It operated under covenant trust and defined boundary.
4. Adam functioned as representative head.
5. The fall would have to be a legal breach because Satan had no rightful dominion to seize.

Chapter 2

# Breach

## What Satan Could Not Take, Man Handed Over

Satan did not take dominion from humanity.
He did not conquer the earth.
He did not overpower God's design.

What Satan could not seize by force, he gained through breach.

This distinction matters because authority lost through deception functions very differently than authority taken through conquest. Conquest implies defeat. Breach implies violation of covenant terms. The fall of man was not the collapse of God's power. It was the misuse of delegated authority within God's legal framework.

## 1. Satan's Position: Outside the Jurisdiction

Before the fall, Satan had no jurisdictional authority in the earth. He was not given dominion. He was not an image bearer. He did not possess stewardship rights. His presence in the garden was not a sign of authority, but of opportunity.

The serpent could speak, but he could not command.
He could suggest, but he could not enforce.
He could tempt, but he could not rule.

This is why his strategy was not aggression, but persuasion.

## 2. Deception as a Legal Strategy

Satan's approach in Genesis 3 reveals his legal limitation. He does not begin with denial of God's existence. He begins with questioning God's word.

"Did God really say…?"

This was not casual curiosity. It was a calculated attempt to undermine the covenantal foundation of authority, which is trust in God's word. Authority remains intact only as long as alignment remains intact. If Satan could induce man to act outside the word of God, he would not need authority to rule. He would gain standing to accuse.

Deception, therefore, was not about knowledge. It was about allegiance.

## 3. Rebellion: The Moment of Breach

When Adam and Eve chose to act contrary to God's command, the issue was not fruit. The issue was jurisdictional violation.

Rebellion in Scripture is not merely disobedience. It is treason against rightful authority. Adam, acting as federal head, violated the terms under which his authority operated. He did not lose dominion immediately. He corrupted its operation.

The authority remained.
The alignment did not.

This is why the immediate consequence was not death by execution, but death by separation.

### 4. The Legal Effects of the Breach

Genesis records several immediate changes, all of them legal in nature:

- Nakedness → exposure where innocence once covered
- Fear → awareness of judgment
- Hiding → loss of confident access
- Blame shifting → fractured responsibility

None of these are random emotions. They are symptoms of guilt entering the human conscience. And where guilt exists, accusation becomes legally viable.

This is the opening Satan required.

### 5. What Man Actually Handed Over

Man did not give Satan ownership of the earth.
Man did not give Satan creative power.
Man did not give Satan sonship.

Man handed over:

- Alignment (obedience to God's word)
- Moral authority (clear conscience)
- Legal standing (innocence)

This is why Satan becomes known as "the accuser." Accusation requires evidence. Evidence requires guilt. Guilt requires breach.

Satan did not gain authority. He gained access through accusation.

### 6. "The Ruler of This World" Explained

When Jesus refers to Satan as "the ruler of this world," He is not affirming Satan's ownership. He is acknowledging a temporary administrative reality: humanity, now under guilt, is susceptible to influence by the accuser.

Satan rules only where:

- guilt is believed
- accusation is accepted
- God's verdict is unknown or rejected

This rulership is not absolute. It is conditional and illegitimate, sustained only by unaddressed breach.

### 7. The Fall Did Not End God's Claim

Crucially, God never relinquished ownership of the earth. The breach did not cancel God's covenantal intent. It necessitated legal remediation.

God did not immediately evict humanity.
God did not destroy the estate.
God did not transfer dominion to Satan.

Instead, God initiated a redemptive legal process, one that would preserve His justice while restoring His original design.

That process would require:

- blood
- substitution
- representation
- and ultimately, a perfect federal head to succeed where Adam failed

**What This Chapter Establishes**

1. Satan lacked authority to take dominion.
2. Deception, not force, produced the fall.
3. Rebellion constituted legal breach, not defeat.
4. Guilt created standing for accusation.
5. Satan's influence operates through access, not ownership.
6. God's redemptive plan begins immediately after breach.

Chapter 3

# Standing

## How Guilt Gave the Accuser a Voice

Authority alone does not determine outcomes in a legal system. Standing does.

Standing is the right to speak, the right to accuse, the right to bring a case before judgment. Before the fall, Satan had no standing in the earth concerning humanity. He could observe, tempt, and deceive, but he could not legitimately accuse because there was no guilt to support the charge.

The breach changed that.

## 1. Guilt as a Legal Condition, Not Just an Emotion

Modern thinking treats guilt as a feeling. Scripture treats guilt as a status. When Adam and Eve sinned, guilt did not merely make them feel bad. It altered their legal position.

In other words, something changed in their standing before God.

This is why their first awareness was not rebellion, but nakedness.

Nakedness was not about bodies. It was about exposure. Innocence had functioned as a covering; guilt removed that covering. Where innocence exists, accusation has no evidence. Where guilt enters, accusation gains footing.

This is the moment Satan required.

### 2. Why Accusation Works Only After Breach

Satan is called "the accuser of the brethren" (Revelation 12:10) not because accusation is his nature, but because accusation is his function within a legal framework. Accusation requires three things:

1. A law
2. A violation
3. Evidence

Before the fall:

- The law existed
- The violation did not
- Evidence was absent

After the fall:

- The law remained
- The violation occurred
- Evidence entered the conscience of man

This is why fear immediately followed guilt. Fear is the awareness of judgment. (Genesis 3:10) Adam and Eve did not fear God before because they had no reason to expect condemnation.

Standing had shifted.

### 3. Conscience: The Internal Witness

One of the most overlooked realities of the fall is the emergence of the conscience as an internal witness. The conscience is not Satan's invention; it is God's design. But after the fall, it became a double-edged instrument.

The conscience testifies:

- to innocence when aligned
- to guilt when violated

Satan does not need to invent accusations when the conscience already confirms them. This is why accusation feels personal. It is reinforced internally.

Standing is strengthened when the accused agrees with the charge.

### 4. Hiding as Legal Admission

When God calls out, "Where are you?" He is not seeking information. He is initiating due process. Adam's hiding is not cowardice. It is an admission that something has changed.

In legal terms:

- innocence approaches authority
- guilt retreats from it

Adam's withdrawal signals awareness of fault. This is why blame shifting immediately follows. Blame is an attempt to redistribute liability.

But liability remains.

### 5. Why Satan's Power Is Tied to Accusation

Satan's influence does not flow from might; it flows from unresolved guilt. His power is not creative. It is procedural. He enforces consequences where breach remains unaddressed.

This is why Scripture consistently ties Satan's activity to:

- accusation
- condemnation
- fear of death
- bondage

All of these require standing. Remove standing, and the accuser loses his voice.

### 6. God's Immediate Legal Response

Here is where the character of God becomes unmistakable.

God does not deny the breach.
God does not dismiss justice.
God does not side with the accuser.

Instead, God immediately moves to address standing.

He questions.
He investigates.
He pronounces judgment.
And then, critically, He introduces blood.

Blood is not emotional symbolism. Blood is legal currency. Life is in the blood (Leviticus 17:11), and blood speaks where words cannot. The shedding of innocent blood introduces a new variable into the case: substitution.

This is not forgiveness yet.
This is covering.

### 7. Standing Is the Battleground of Redemption

From this point forward, the entire redemptive narrative will revolve around one issue: standing before God.

- Who has the right to accuse?
- On what basis?
- Can guilt be covered?
- Can guilt be removed?
- Can standing be restored permanently?

Until standing is resolved, dominion cannot be restored. Authority without standing collapses under accusation. This is why God's solution would require more than instruction. It would require a legal exchange sufficient to silence the accuser entirely.

---

**What This Chapter Establishes**

1. Guilt is a legal condition, not merely a feeling.
2. Standing determines the power of accusation.
3. Satan's influence depends on unresolved guilt.
4. Conscience functions as internal witness.
5. Hiding and fear signal loss of standing.
6. God responds immediately to address standing through blood.
7. Redemption will hinge on resolving guilt, not suppressing behavior.

Chapter 4

# Covering

## Why Blood Was Introduced but the Case Was Not Closed

God's response to the fall was immediate, deliberate, and legally precise. He did not ignore the breach, and He did not allow accusation to operate unchecked. Instead, He introduced a mechanism that would temporarily stabilize the case while pointing forward to a permanent resolution.

That mechanism was covering.

### 1. Genesis 3:21 – God's First Legal Action

Genesis records a critical moment often read too quickly:

"The Lord God made garments of skin for Adam and his wife and clothed them."

This is not poetic detail. This is legal intervention.

For garments of skin to exist, blood had to be shed. An innocent life was taken, not because God delights in death, but because death had already entered the system through breach. Blood was introduced as a countermeasure, not to erase the violation, but to address exposure.

God did not accept Adam's fig leaves. Human effort cannot resolve legal guilt. Self-covering does not silence accusation. Only blood, representing life, can respond to death's claim.

### 2. Why Covering Was Necessary

Covering addressed three immediate problems created by the breach:

1. Exposure – nakedness represented vulnerability before judgment
2. Standing – guilt had created legal footing for accusation
3. Access – fear had fractured confident relationship

The blood did not remove guilt from existence, but it covered it from view. In legal terms, the case was stayed, not dismissed.

Covering means:

- guilt exists
- accusation is restrained
- judgment is delayed

This distinction is essential. Covering manages consequences; it does not eliminate cause.

### 3. Why Animals Were Used

Animals were not chosen randomly. They were innocent, unknowing, and not morally accountable. Their lives could function as substitutes, but not as equals.

This limitation matters.

A substitute can:

- absorb consequence
- provide temporary relief
- symbolize payment

But a substitute cannot:

- fully represent a moral agent
- permanently restore standing
- end accusation

Animals could cover humanity, but they could not replace humanity in the legal sense.

**4. Covering Preserved God's Justice and Mercy**

Covering allowed God to remain just without executing immediate judgment and merciful without dismissing the law. It preserved the integrity of the system while buying time for a greater solution.

This is why God does not remove Adam and Eve from the earth. Dominion remains fractured but intact. Humanity is not erased. The redemptive process begins inside the existing jurisdiction.

Covering is God holding the case open, not closing it.

**5. The Continuation of Covering – Levitical Law**

The pattern introduced in Genesis becomes formalized in Leviticus:

"It is the blood that makes atonement for the soul." (Leviticus 17:11)

Atonement literally means "to cover."

The sacrifices:

- addressed guilt annually
- restrained accusation temporarily
- restored access to the community
- maintained covenant continuity

But repetition reveals insufficiency.

Anything that must be repeated is, by definition, incomplete.

The writer of Hebrews later affirms this limitation: "It is impossible for the blood of bulls and goats to take away sins." (Hebrews 10:4)

### 6. Why Accusation Continued

If blood was applied, why did accusation persist?

Because covering hides guilt; it does not eliminate it.

This is why:

- sacrifices were repeated
- priests died and were replaced
- consciences were never fully cleansed
- fear of judgment remained

Satan's standing was reduced but not destroyed. He could not condemn outright, but he could remind, pressure, and intimidate.

Covering restricted Satan's reach.
It did not revoke his access.

### 7. Covering Was a Signpost, Not a Solution

Every sacrifice preached a message the system itself could not fulfill:

"Something greater is required."

Blood was necessary, but animal blood was insufficient. The problem was not blood itself; it was representation. The law required a payment equal to the offense. Humanity required a representative capable of standing fully in its place.

Until then, the system functioned on mercy deferred.

---

**What This Chapter Establishes**

1. God introduced blood immediately after breach.
2. Covering restrained accusation but did not remove guilt.
3. Human effort cannot resolve legal exposure.
4. Animal sacrifice functioned as temporary substitution.
5. Covering preserved justice while delaying judgment.
6. Repetition revealed incompleteness.
7. A greater representative was required to close the case.

Chapter 5

# Representation

## Why the Case Required a Man, Not Another Animal

Covering restrained the consequences of the breach, but it did not resolve the case. For the legal matter to be closed, the system required something far more specific than blood alone. It required proper representation.

In any just legal system, the penalty must be addressed by a party equal to the offense. Substitution is only valid if the substitute is legally qualified to stand in the place of the accused. This is where animal sacrifice, by design, reached its limit.

### 1. Representation Is the Core Requirement of Justice

The original breach did not occur in the animal kingdom. It occurred within human jurisdiction. Adam was not acting as a private individual. He was acting as a representative head of humanity. Therefore, the resolution could not be assigned to a lesser category of being.

Justice requires:

- equal nature
- equal jurisdiction
- equal accountability

Animals could die, but they could not stand trial. They lacked moral agency. They could absorb consequence, but they could not legally answer the charge.

This is why the law itself pointed beyond them (Hebrews 10:1).

### 2. Why Angels Were Never an Option

Angels were never candidates for substitution.

They:

- do not share human nature
- do not operate within human jurisdiction
- were not assigned dominion over the earth

Even a sinless angel would lack standing to represent humanity. Representation is not about purity alone. It is about legal equivalence. The offense was committed by man; therefore, only a man could resolve it.

Heaven could not fix earth's legal problem by bypassing earth.

### 3. Federal Headship Revisited

Adam's role as federal head created the scope of the problem and also revealed the scope of the solution.

Scripture treats Adam not merely as the first sinner, but as the first representative (Romans 5:18–19). His obedience or disobedience carried collective consequence. This establishes a critical principle:

What one authorized man does can affect many.

This is not unfair. It is how authority functions.

Therefore, the only way to reverse Adam's failure was not by undoing history, but by introducing a new federal head, one who could act lawfully within the same jurisdiction and succeed where Adam failed.

## 4. The Law's Silent Demand: A Perfect Man

The law did not explicitly say, "A perfect man must come."

But the structure demanded it.

- The offense was human.
- The authority was human.
- The guilt rested on humanity.

Therefore:

- The payment must be human.
- The obedience must be human.
- The standing must be human.

At the same time, the representative would need to be without guilt, or else he would require a substitute for himself. This creates an apparent impossibility: every human born after Adam inherits the condition of guilt (Romans 5:12).

So, the case stands unresolved unless a man could enter the system without inheriting Adam's breach.

## 5. Why Birth Matters Legally

This is why the incarnation is not optional theology. It is legal necessity.

Jesus was not created; He was born.
He did not appear; He entered.
He did not bypass humanity; He assumed it.

Born of a woman, Jesus lawfully entered human jurisdiction (Galatians 4:4). Conceived by the Spirit, He entered without inherited guilt.

This is not mystical language. It is legal precision.

Jesus qualified as:

- fully human (equal representation)
- without sin (no personal liability)
- under the law (subject to its demands)

For the first time since Adam, a man existed who could stand before the law without requiring covering.

### 6. Obedience as Legal Counteraction

Where Adam's breach occurred through disobedience, the resolution required perfect obedience. This is why Jesus' life matters as much as His death.

Every act of obedience:

- upheld the law
- maintained alignment
- preserved standing

Jesus did not only die for sin. He lived without it. His obedience built a legal record capable of replacing Adam's failure (Philippians 2:8).

This is the foundation of exchange.

### 7. The Setup for the Lamb

By the time Jesus reaches the cross, the requirements are finally met:

- a man
- a representative
- without guilt
- with authority
- capable of substitution

Now, and only now, can blood do more than cover.

Now blood can remove.

---

**What This Chapter Establishes**

1. Legal resolution requires equal representation.
2. Animals could substitute temporarily but not resolve permanently.
3. Angels lack jurisdiction to represent humanity.
4. Adam's role as federal head necessitated a new federal head.
5. The law demanded a perfect man.
6. Jesus' birth was legally essential, not symbolic.
7. Obedience established a qualifying record.
8. The stage is set for final exchange.

Chapter 6

# The Lamb

## Why "The Lamb of God" Is Legal Language, Not Poetic Metaphor

When John the Baptist declared, "Behold, the Lamb of God" (John 1:29), he was not offering devotional poetry. He was announcing a legal resolution centuries in the making. That statement carried courtroom weight, covenant memory, and jurisdictional finality. To understand the cross, we must understand the Lamb, not as symbolism, but as substitution with standing.

### 1. The Lamb Was Always About Representation

From the beginning, the lamb was never just an animal. It was a legal proxy. In the sacrificial system, the lamb functioned as a substitute whose life stood temporarily in the place of another. But more importantly, the lamb operated within a framework of representation, not mere ritual.

This becomes unmistakable at Passover.

### 2. Passover: The Household Principle

In Exodus 12, God does not instruct Israel to sacrifice one lamb per person. He commands one lamb per household. This is not incidental. It establishes a legal principle that will later be fulfilled in Christ.

The lamb:

- represented the entire house
- absorbed judgment on behalf of all inside

- created a protected jurisdiction marked by blood

The blood was not applied to individuals. It was applied to the doorpost, the point of entry and authority. Anyone inside the house was legally covered, regardless of age, merit, or awareness.

This is not individual morality. It is corporate representation.

### 3. Blood as Jurisdiction Marker

The blood on the door did not cleanse the people; it marked the house. The destroyer did not inspect behavior. He responded to blood applied in obedience (Exodus 12:13).

This distinction matters. Judgment did not pass over Israel because they were righteous. It passed over because blood was present where God instructed it to be.

Blood defined jurisdiction.

### 4. "The Lamb of God": Ownership and Authority

When John calls Jesus "the Lamb of God," he is identifying:

- the source of the lamb (God, not man)
- the scope of the lamb (God's household, not one nation)
- the authority behind the lamb (divine initiative)

Jesus is not merely a lamb provided by God. He is God's Lamb, chosen, authorized, and presented by God Himself. This means the sacrifice is not reactive. It is intentional and final.

## 5. From Substitution to Identification

Animal lambs substituted temporarily. They stood in the place of sinners but remained separate from them. Jesus does something fundamentally different.

He does not merely substitute. He identifies.

By becoming human, Jesus does not stand beside humanity. He stands as humanity's representative. His death is not the death of an animal for a man. It is the death of a man for men.

This is why Scripture can say:

- "In Him" we died (Romans 6:6)
- "In Him" we were buried (Romans 6:4)
- "In Him" we were raised (Ephesians 2:6)

Identification replaces substitution.

## 6. Why the Lamb Ends the System

The sacrificial system required repetition because it lacked permanence. Jesus' sacrifice ends repetition because it satisfies representation, obedience, and payment simultaneously.

- The Lamb is human → equal representation
- The Lamb is sinless → no personal liability
- The Lamb is obedient → qualifying record
- The Lamb is offered once → final payment

The system does not evolve. It concludes (Hebrews 10:12).

This is why the veil tears. This is why the altar goes silent. This is why no further blood is required.

The law is not bypassed. It is fulfilled (Matthew 5:17).

### 7. The Lamb and the Household of God

The Lamb of God represents more than individuals. It establishes a new household. Anyone who enters Christ enters the house marked by His blood.

This is not metaphorical belonging. It is legal adoption (Ephesians 1:5).

Inside this household:

- accusation loses standing
- guilt loses authority
- judgment has already passed

The blood has been applied.

---

**What This Chapter Establishes**

1. "Lamb" is legal terminology rooted in representation.
2. Passover established the household principle.
3. Blood marks jurisdiction, not behavior.
4. Jesus is God's authorized Lamb.
5. Identification replaces substitution.
6. Repetition ends because the payment is final.
7. Entry into Christ is entry into a protected household.

Chapter 7

# The Verdict

## From Covering to Cancellation

The cross was not a moment of emotional relief.
It was not a spiritual gesture.
It was not symbolic suffering.

The cross was the rendering of a verdict.

Everything before it prepared the case. Everything after it enforces the outcome. When Jesus declared, "It is finished" (John 19:30), He was not expressing exhaustion. He was issuing a legal pronouncement. The matter that had remained open since Genesis was closed in full.

## 1. "It Is Finished" as Legal Language

The phrase Jesus used, *tetelestai*, was a term commonly written across legal and financial documents to signify payment in full. It did not mean "ended." It meant completed with no remaining obligation.

This is critical.

Covering delays judgment.
Cancellation eliminates liability.

At the cross, the case moves from deferred judgment to final resolution.

## 2. The Record of Debt

Paul articulates the verdict clearly:

"Having canceled the record of debt that stood against us with its legal demands, He set it aside, nailing it to the cross." (Colossians 2:14)

The "record of debt" is not vague spiritual guilt. It is a legal document, a ledger of violations that provided standing for accusation. As long as this record existed, Satan could accuse lawfully.

At the cross:

- the record was canceled
- the evidence was removed
- the standing collapsed

There is no case without a record.

**3. Disarming the Accuser**

The next verse clarifies the consequence:

"He disarmed the rulers and authorities and made a public spectacle of them…" (Colossians 2:15)

Disarming does not mean destruction. It means removal of legal right. Satan was not annihilated; he was stripped of standing.

The weapon removed was accusation (Revelation 12:10).

Without accusation:

- condemnation loses force
- fear of judgment dissolves
- bondage breaks

This is why Satan's power after the cross is persuasive, not authoritative.

#### 4. Blood That Speaks Better

Hebrews declares that Jesus' blood "speaks a better word" (Hebrews 12:24). This is not mystical language. It is courtroom imagery. Blood testifies. Abel's blood cried out for justice (Genesis 4:10). Jesus' blood cries out justice satisfied.

The law heard the blood.
Justice responded.
The verdict was rendered.

This is why no further sacrifice is permitted. Any attempt to add to the blood of Christ is not humility. It is denial of finality.

#### 5. The End of Repetition

Hebrews states it plainly:

"By one sacrifice He has perfected forever those who are being sanctified." (Hebrews 10:14)

Forever is not progressive language. It is permanent status.

The system of repetition ends because:

- guilt has been removed
- conscience has been cleansed
- standing has been restored

Covering kept sin out of sight.
Cancellation removes sin from the record.

#### 6. What Actually Changed at the Cross

The cross did not change God's disposition toward humanity. God was never hostile, hesitant, or reluctant. The cross changed human standing before the law.

What changed:

- guilt → removed
- accusation → silenced
- access → restored
- authority → reclaimed
- adoption → secured

What did not change:

- God's love
- God's intent
- God's ownership

The cross did not make God willing to forgive. It made forgiveness legally enforceable.

### 7. Why Believers Still Feel Accusation

This is the tension many live in. Accusation still speaks, not because it is valid, but because it is familiar. The enemy continues to rehearse charges that have already been dismissed.

The verdict has been rendered.

The question is not whether the case is closed.
The question is whether believers will live from the verdict or from the memory of the charges.

---

**What This Chapter Establishes**

1. "It is finished" is a legal declaration of full payment.
2. The record of debt was canceled, not suppressed.
3. Accusation lost standing at the cross.
4. Satan was disarmed, not destroyed.
5. Christ's blood testifies justice satisfied.
6. Repetition ended because the case was closed.
7. Believers now live from a verdict, not toward one.

Chapter 8

# Enforcement

## Why the Verdict Must Be Stood On, Not Re-Litigated

A verdict can be legally final and still practically unenforced.

Courts do not re-try settled cases, but individuals can live as though the ruling never happened. This is the condition many believers experience after the cross. Not because the verdict is unclear, but because the mind and conscience have not been aligned with it.

The work of Christ settled the case.
The work of faith is standing in that settlement.

### 1. The Difference Between Verdict and Experience

The cross changed reality objectively.
Believers often struggle subjectively.

This gap is not spiritual failure. It is misalignment.

The verdict declares:

- no remaining debt
- no standing for accusation
- restored access
- restored authority

But experience is shaped by what is believed, rehearsed, and enforced. Satan cannot reopen the case, but he can attempt to rehearse dismissed charges.

## 2. Accusation After Acquittal

Accusation does not stop automatically when a verdict is issued. It stops when the accused refuses to accept illegitimate claims.

Post-cross accusation works by:

- replaying past failures
- re-presenting forgiven sin
- inducing self-condemnation
- provoking performance-based righteousness

This is not legal authority.
It is psychological pressure.

The enemy is not acting as a judge. He is acting as a discredited prosecutor hoping the accused will self-incriminate.

There is now no condemnation for those who are in Christ Jesus (Romans 8:1).

## 3. The Role of the Mind in Enforcement

Paul's instruction to "renew the mind" is not motivational language. It is legal alignment (Romans 12:2). The mind must be brought into agreement with the verdict already rendered.

Failure to renew the mind results in:

- striving instead of standing
- confession as fear instead of agreement
- repentance driven by shame instead of truth

Renewal does not create freedom.
It recognizes it.

### 4. Standing vs. Striving

Standing is passive in posture but active in belief.
Striving attempts to achieve what has already been granted.

Standing says:

- "The debt is canceled."
- "The blood has spoken."
- "The case is closed."

Striving says:

- "I must prove my sincerity."
- "I must earn restored access."
- "I must cover myself again."

Striving re-litigates the case.
Standing enforces the verdict.

### 5. Why Re-Confession Can Become Re-Litigation

Confession is biblical (1 John 1:9), but only when it agrees with the truth.

Confession that says:

"I sinned, and I thank You that the blood of Christ has already addressed this."

is enforcement.

Confession that says:

"I sinned, and I hope God will forgive me again."

is denial of finality.

The difference is not humility.
It is belief.

### 6. Enforcement Is Agreement With Heaven

Heaven is not reconsidering the case.
Heaven is not waiting for more payment.
Heaven is not tallying infractions.

The courtroom is silent.

Enforcement happens when believers:

- reject accusation
- refuse shame
- stand on blood-bought identity
- operate from sonship, not probation

This is not arrogance.
It is alignment with reality.

### 7. Faith as Legal Confidence

Faith is not optimism.
Faith is confidence in a settled matter.

Faith says:

"If God has justified me, no accusation has authority."

This is why Scripture asks:

"Who will bring a charge against God's elect?" (Romans 8:33)

The answer is not "no one will try."
The answer is no one will succeed.

**What This Chapter Establishes**

1. Verdicts require enforcement to shape experience.
2. Accusation after the cross lacks legal standing.
3. The mind is the primary enforcement arena.
4. Standing enforces; striving re-litigates.
5. Misaligned confession undermines assurance.
6. Heaven has closed the case.
7. Faith is agreement with the verdict, not hope for leniency.

Chapter 9

# Dominion Restored

## What Authority Looks Like After the Verdict

Authority does not return the same way it was lost.

It is not reclaimed through force, effort, or intensity. Dominion is restored through standing, not striving. After the verdict, authority no longer flows from innocence maintained, but from righteousness granted.

This distinction is everything.

## 1. Authority After the Cross Is Not Conditional

Before the fall, authority was maintained through obedience. After the cross, authority is exercised through identity.

This is why Scripture says:

"As many as received Him, to them He gave the right to become children of God." (John 1:12)

Authority now flows from sonship, not probation.

The believer does not wake up each day trying to qualify for authority. Authority is exercised because qualification has already been settled by the blood.

## 2. Reigning in Life, Not Managing Sin

Paul's language is deliberate:

"Those who receive abundance of grace and the gift of righteousness will reign in life through the One, Jesus Christ." (Romans 5:17)

Reigning is not about controlling circumstances. It is about operating from settled standing. A believer who understands the verdict does not obsess over sin management; he lives from restored alignment.

Sin loses dominion when guilt loses authority.

### 3. The Proper Understanding of "Resist the Devil"

Scripture commands believers to resist the devil (James 4:7), but resistance is not combat. It is denial of access.

To resist means:

- to refuse agreement
- to deny standing
- to reject illegitimate claims

The devil flees not because he is overpowered, but because he is unwelcomed.

You do not resist an intruder by debating ownership of the house. You enforce the deed.

### 4. Dominion Without Fear

Fear is incompatible with dominion. Fear signals uncertainty of standing. This is why fear diminishes authority. It creates hesitation, retreat, and overreaction.

Perfect love casts out fear (1 John 4:18) because love confirms belonging.

A son does not fear eviction.

**5. Authority Flows From Rest**

The restored dominion promised in Christ does not produce anxiety. It produces rest. Rest is not passivity; it is confidence in completion.

God rested after creation not because He was tired, but because the work was finished (Genesis 2:2). Likewise, believers operate from rest because the work of redemption is complete.

Rest is not inactivity. It is stability.

**6. Sonship vs Servitude**

Servants obey to avoid punishment.
Sons operate from inheritance.

This is why legalism collapses authority. Legalism reintroduces probation where adoption has already occurred. Sonship restores dominion because it restores confidence of belonging.

The enemy fears sons more than servants because sons know where they stand.

**7. Dominion Is Not Control, It Is Alignment**

Restored dominion does not mean believers dominate others. It means they operate aligned with heaven's rule. Authority is exercised through truth, peace, obedience, and confidence, not coercion.

Jesus demonstrated perfect dominion while washing feet (John 13:14-15).

That is restored authority.

**What This Chapter Establishes**

1. Authority after the cross flows from sonship.
2. Dominion is exercised from standing, not striving.
3. Resistance is denial of illegitimate access.
4. Fear undermines authority.
5. Rest is the posture of finished work.
6. Sonship restores confidence and clarity.
7. Dominion expresses alignment, not control.

## Chapter 10
# Living the Exchange

### From Verdict to Embodied Reality

A verdict that is understood but not lived remains theoretical.

The purpose of revelation is not information. It is alignment. The Great Exchange was not given so believers could explain salvation more accurately. It was given so believers could live free without confusion, confident without arrogance, obedient without fear.

This chapter is not about adding effort. It is about removing distortion.

### 1. Living From the Verdict, Not Toward It

Many believers live as if salvation is something being maintained rather than something already secured. This posture subtly turns faith into probation.

Scripture declares, "There is therefore now no condemnation for those who are in Christ Jesus." (Romans 8:1)

Living from the verdict means:

- obedience flows from identity
- repentance flows from truth
- discipline flows from love
- growth flows from safety

The believer is not working to remain accepted. He is learning to live as one who already is.

### 2. Repentance Without Re-Litigation

Repentance after the cross is not courtroom pleading. It is relational realignment.

True repentance says:
"I agree with God about what this behavior contradicts, and I return to alignment."

False repentance says:
"I hope God will forgive me again."

The difference is subtle but decisive. One enforces the verdict. The other questions it.

Repentance does not reopen guilt.
It restores clarity.

As Scripture teaches, "Godly sorrow produces repentance leading to salvation, not to be regretted." (2 Corinthians 7:10)

### 3. Confession as Agreement, Not Fear

Confession is powerful when it agrees with truth.

"If we confess our sins, He is faithful and just to forgive us our sins and to cleanse us from all unrighteousness." (1 John 1:9)

Notice the word just. Forgiveness is not emotional leniency. It is legal consistency with what Christ has accomplished.

Confession that enforces the exchange:

- "I sinned, and the blood of Christ has already addressed this."
- "This behavior does not define me."
- "I return to who I am."

Confession driven by fear seeks relief.
Confession grounded in truth enforces freedom.

**4. Identity Based Obedience**

Obedience after the exchange is not compliance. It is expression.

Sons obey because they belong.
Servants obey because they fear loss.

This is why the New Testament emphasizes transformation over regulation. The law demanded behavior. Grace produces alignment of desire.

The exchange did not remove responsibility.
It removed condemnation as motivation.

**5. Walking Free Without Denial**

Freedom does not mean denial of weakness. It means weakness is no longer fatal. Failure does not threaten standing.

Hebrews declares that we may "come boldly to the throne of grace." (Hebrews 4:16)

Boldness is not arrogance. It is confidence in access.

Growth becomes honest because shame no longer governs the process. The believer can confront sin without panic because the verdict is settled.

Freedom produces courage.

**6. The Daily Enforcement Posture**

Living the exchange daily means:

- rejecting accusation quickly
- refusing to rehearse forgiven sin
- standing on identity when emotions fluctuate
- allowing discipline without shame
- choosing truth over familiarity

The enemy's strategy after the cross is repetition. The believer's strategy is refusal.

### 7. The Exchange Completed and Applied

The Great Exchange was not partial.

- Adam's failure → Christ's obedience
- Guilt → righteousness
- Accusation → acquittal
- Distance → access
- Servitude → sonship

Nothing remains unpaid.
Nothing remains undecided.
Nothing remains provisional.

The only remaining question is not legal. It is relational:

Will we live as those who have been acquitted, or as those still awaiting a verdict?

## Final Establishment

The cross did not make salvation possible.
It made salvation final.

The blood did not begin a process.
It concluded a case.

The exchange is complete.
The verdict is rendered.
The authority is restored.

Now, the invitation is simple:

Live like it is true.

Legal Summary Thesis

# The Great Exchange – Final Findings

This work has established a single, cohesive legal reality:

1. God lawfully delegated dominion to humanity at creation. Authority in the earth was granted, not symbolic, and functioned under covenant alignment.
2. Satan never possessed original authority over humanity or the earth. His influence entered only through deception induced breach, not conquest.
3. The fall constituted a legal breach, not a defeat of God. Guilt entered the human conscience, creating standing for accusation.
4. Blood was introduced immediately as legal response, beginning with Genesis 3:21. This blood provided covering, restraining judgment but not closing the case.
5. The sacrificial system formalized covering, but repetition proved insufficiency. Animal blood could manage exposure but could not remove guilt or permanently silence accusation.
6. Justice required equal representation.
   The offense was human; therefore, only a sinless human representative could resolve the case.
7. Jesus Christ entered human jurisdiction lawfully, born of a woman, conceived without inherited guilt, and living in perfect obedience under the law.
8. Jesus functioned as the final federal head, succeeding where Adam failed and qualifying as the Lamb.

9. At the cross, the record of debt was canceled, not suppressed. The legal evidence supporting accusation was removed.
10. Satan was disarmed and stripped of standing, not destroyed. Accusation lost authority. Influence remains only through deception.
11. The verdict was rendered once and for all.
The case is closed. Repetition is prohibited. Re-litigation is illegitimate.
12. Believers now live from a verdict, not toward one. Authority is restored through sonship. Dominion flows from standing. Enforcement is alignment.

**Final Legal Conclusion**

The Great Exchange is complete.
The debt is paid.
The record is cleared.
The verdict is final.
The authority is restored.

Any continued accusation operates outside lawful standing and derives its force only from ignorance, not legitimacy.

## Closing Prayer

Father God,

We acknowledge You as Creator, Judge, Redeemer, and Father.

We thank You that You did not abandon justice, nor withhold mercy. We thank You that through Jesus Christ, You resolved what humanity could not.

We receive the finished work of the cross, not as theory, not as tradition, but as truth.

We thank You that the blood of Jesus has spoken and that its testimony still stands.

We renounce every lie that suggests the case is still open.
We reject every voice of accusation that contradicts Your verdict.

Align our minds with what Heaven has declared.
Teach us to stand where Christ has seated us.

Let our obedience flow from sonship, not fear.
Let our repentance flow from truth, not shame.

We rest in what You have completed.
We honor the exchange.
We live from the verdict.

In the name of Jesus Christ,
Amen.

## Declaration

The Great Exchange

I declare that the case against me is closed.
The record of debt has been canceled.
The blood of Jesus has spoken on my behalf.

I am no longer covered. I am acquitted.
I am no longer striving. I am standing.
I am no longer accused. I am justified.

I reject every illegitimate charge.
I refuse to rehearse forgiven sin.
I stand in restored authority as a child of God.

I live from righteousness granted, not earned.
I resist accusation by denying its standing.
I walk in dominion through alignment, not fear.

The exchange is complete.
The verdict is final.
I live accordingly.

Glory to God.

www.ingramcontent.com/pod-product-compliance
Lightning Source LLC
La Vergne TN
LVHW010835120826
845149LV00016B/2741